# UNIFORM AND DRESS

of the

## ARMY AND NAVY

of the

### Confederate States of America

Introduction by

R I C H A R D   H A R W E L L

*NEW YORK*

St Martin's Press, Inc.

THE FIRST EDITION, DEDICATED TO THE COMPANY OF
MILITARY COLLECTORS AND HISTORIANS, COPYRIGHT 1952 BY RAY RILING
THIS REVISED EDITION, WITH INTRODUCTION BY
RICHARD B. HARWELL, COPYRIGHT 1960, BY RAY RILING
LIBRARY OF CONGRESS CATALOG CARD NUMBER 60-16421
PRINTED IN THE UNITED STATES OF AMERICA

A. M. D. G.

*and*

*For Floyd Cammack*

*and*

*Peter Demery*

*my co-workers in the*

*world of books.*

R. B. H.

# INTRODUCTION

Confederate soldiers marched to war in high style as well as high spirits. What the well dressed officer would wear was a matter of considerable concern to the dandies who volunteered in the spring of 1861 for what they expected to be a short, brilliant, and decisive campaign against the Yankees. Although the uniforms of the regulations existed for only a limited number of officers and men, they did exist. This printing as a unit of three rare Confederate publications about uniforms is a truly worthwhile contribution to our records of the Confederacy.

By 1861 the military spirit had been rife in the South for a full generation. Local militia companies and volunteer drilling units had collected to their standards the élite of nearly every Southern community. Each company had selected or designed its own uniforms. Though these uniforms ranged through an infinite variety — from the swash-buckling Zouave pantaloons and blouses of the New Orleans Tiger Rifles through the green of the Mobile Emerald Guards, the yellow of the Tennessee Yellow Jackets, and the red and black of North Carolina's Granville Rifles to the nattily conservative outfits of the Richmond Blues — the most usual uniform color was cadet gray. Considering its frequency of use, its comparative availability, and its serviceability, it is not surprising that, when a General Order designating the official Confederate uniforms was issued on June 6, 1861, cadet gray was the color prescribed for them.

Henry Hotze, a private in the Mobile Cadets in 1861 who later edited *The Index,* the Confederate propaganda journal published in London, wrote in his "Three Months in the Confederate Army" (first published in *The Index* in 1862) that a new "simple and serviceable campaign uniform"[1] had been secured for the Cadets and noted the contrast between the company of "city-bred gentlemen" and the volunteers from the country districts. "In their green hunting shirts," he commented, "for the country companies have not yet had time to uniform themselves, they have much the appearance of good-humoured savages."[2]

The Confederate economy was not equipped to supply enough cadet gray cloth to clothe an army in short order, and its importation was slow and costly. Though the issue of clothing to soldiers was authorized practice, it never sufficed to fill the needs of the men and soon diminished as efforts at local manufacture were reduced by the hazards of war and importations severely curtailed by the ever-tightening Federal blockade.

1. Henry Hotze, *Three Months in the Confederate Army* (University, Ala., 1952), p. 13.
2. *Ibid.,* p. 14.

Home industry and the volunteer efforts of Southern women combined to keep the Confederate soldiers outfitted. Hotze described the lighthearted work of one volunteer group at Montgomery in the early days of the war:

> On the way to town is a little Baptist Church, of which the ladies of the city have taken possession, and there they lie in ambush, sallying forth and capturing the groups of soldiers that loiter townward, to offer them the services of their busy needles. Our uniforms, though simple, were made by the best tailors, and as yet not a button has had time to come off. But the fair patriots will not be disappointed, and so each one of us has been presented with a sort of fatigue cap of red flannel, with a jaunty yellow tassel, which the boys now wear under their kepips [kepis], in honour of the donors. We have also a sort of havelock of white linen, not unlike the hood of a Sister of Charity, to protect us against the hot sun, imitated from the pictures of Zouaves in the Algerian war; and when our wags wear red cap, kepips [kepis], and hood, all at the same time, the effect is irresistibly comical. [3]

Such lighthearted efforts at helping the soldiers marked the beginning of the war; soon the work of the women at home was a real need if the soldiers were to be kept clothed.

In August 1861, less than two weeks after he had arrived in Virginia as a private in the Second Georgia Infantry Battalion, Henry L. Graves was writing to his father in Newton County, Georgia:

> I wish that Ma would send me a coat; let her make it of that gray woolen cloth she once made me a hunting coat from, or something of the same color. The cloth [for uniforms] was furnished to us in Macon and it only cost 3 dollars for me to have a suit made. I had the pants made but had not enough money for the coat. Ma can fit it by any of my coats. It must be a jacket buttoning all the way up in front, military fashion, with a short collar designed to stand up; buttons either brass or silver, oval shape, nearly half inch in diameter; put a short piece of white tape ¼ inch wide upon the shoulder, running from front to back. Let it be warm; pockets inside and on both sides. [4]

By the next August this comparatively wealthy young Georgian was writing home: "I am looking out most anxiously for my box. I am needing a new supply of under clothing and hope the box will have one or two good shirts, pair of drawers, socks, etc." and "My pants are wearing out, and [I] wish you would please make me a new pair, and send me if possible, from the same material, or at least send me a patch or two, or I will have to patch dark pants with a white piece." [5]

In an excellent chapter, "From Finery to Tatters," in his *The Life of Johnny Reb* Bell I. Wiley cites incident after incident of how soldiers were supplied from home. Typical is his quotation from a letter by E. P. Becton, a Virginia soldier, to his wife. "I sold my pants, vest, shoes, & drawers for sixtyone dollars so you see I am flush again . . . You will have to make me more pants and drawers, if you can raise the material make two pair of pants & four pair of drawers & I will have A pair of pants & two pair of

3. *Ibid.,* p. 16.
4. Henry Lea Graves to Iverson Lea Graves, Sewell's Point, Va., August 21, 1861; Graves Letters, Southern Historical Collections, University of North Carolina, Chapel Hill, N. C.
5. H. L. Graves to Hattie Dutton, Petersburg, Va., August 7, 1862.

drawers for sale in that way will get mine clear . . . if you could make up a good supply of pants vests shirts and drawers, I could be detailed out to come after them." [6]

Uniforms were always less important than fighting—except in such rare incidents as when Fitz Lee captured Federal General John Pope's cloak and hat, or when J. E. B. Stuart lost his own hat and plume to that same Federal officer. Neither side ever brought complete uniformity into the attire of its armies. Robert Underwood Johnson and Clarence Clough Buell commented in a note in their classic anthology, *Battles and Leaders of the Civil War,* on the variety of uniforms at the beginning of the war:

> The battle of Bull Run was notable in a minor way for the variety of uniforms worn on both sides — a variety greater than was shown in any later engagement. The Federal blue had not yet been issued, and the troops wore either the uniforms of their militia organizations (including various patterns of Zouave dress) or those furnished by their several States. The Confederate uniforms exhibited similar variety; some regiments were in citizens' dress, and several of the general officers who had been in the old service — including, we are informed, Generals Johnston, Beauregard, and Longstreet — still wore the dress of the United States Army. [7]

Just as the uniforms of the Confederate Army were in the general style of military dress of the period (with considerable French influence), so were the uniforms of the Confederate Navy typical of the time, although the regulations substituted black and gray for traditional navy blue. Sailors, however, freely wore blue, and their uniforms deviated as fully from those designated by regulations as did those of the soldiers.

Less survives concerning naval uniforms than army uniforms. The Graves Letters are a revealing source of information about naval uniforms in the latter part of the war, for Iverson Dutton Graves, brother of the Henry Graves already quoted, joined the Confederate Naval Squadron at Savannah in 1864. Henry Graves, then a Marine officer stationed with the Savannah Squadron, wrote his father in March of that year:

> His [Dutton's] rank as Master's Mate entitles him to rank with Midshipmen, and to associate with the other officers of the ship. The life is far preferable to the ranks of the army on account of its comparative freedom from exposure to the weather . . . Dutt will need a new uniform suit. A dress suit here would cost him about $500. If my Mother can get some light grey jeans made, and send the cloth down, it will do very well, and he can get it cut and made here for a moderate sum. His pay (about 45 dols. per month) will not be sufficient to support him unless he stints, from month's end to month's end. [8]

Dutton himself noted in a letter to his mother on April 24: "I wish you would look among my clothes and see if that pair of sailor pants are fit for wear. If so, please send them with as many more white pants as you can find, blue jackets and white pants you know are regular sailor style." [9] The next week Henry wrote her: "Now of Dutt and his clothes — . . . The striped cloth would not do well, especially as it is getting quite hot here. He needs gray." [10] On June 13, Dutton wrote: "I am much obliged to you for the

6. Bell Irvin Wiley, *The Life of Johnny Reb* (Indianapolis, [1943]), p. 114.
7. Century Magazine, *Battles and Leaders of the Civil War* (New-York, [c. 1884-88]), I, 167.
8. H. L. Graves to I. L. Graves, [Savannah, Ga., undated (March, 1864)].
9. Iverson Dutton Graves to Mrs. Sarah (Dutton) Graves, *CSS Savannah,* April 24, 1864.
10. H. L. Graves to Mrs. S. D. Graves, Savannah, Ga., April 29, 1864.

cloth. I am having it made up and it is all ready except the buttons. The pants are too small at the foot; except [for] that they fit very nicely. Jeans is so seldom worn here that I will be alone in my glory. I will try to draw some cloth from the department and think I may possibly get some after a while. The coat costs fifty dollars — a pretty good price for making only. I would like to have made some white pants if you can get the material, and two or three white vests." [11]

Dutton Graves fled Savannah with the rest of the Naval Squadron when the city fell to General William Tecumseh Sherman in December 1864. The fate of his laboriously acquired wardrobe is told in his letter home of January 20, 1865:

> You should have seen me as I started out; to have appreciated the woe begone face and dismall groans that would have greeted you as we sloped. On Tuesday night the city fell . . . On Wednesday night commenced our troubles. An order was issued to leave by 8 o'clock so forthwith I buckled on my armor, made a little knapsack, put in two changes of clothes, strapped on a blanket, and shawl, and announced myself in readiness. How light the load felt then; I thought I could walk a thousand miles with it and not tire. . . . We were about six miles distant when our ship blew up, and you have no idea what a sad blow it was to me. Thinks I, there goes my pleasant quarters, my good clothes, my good warm overcoat, and I am forever cut off from Savannah and the hope of ever making myself agreeable to the Savannah girls; my heart sank within me, my limbs ached, my load was terribly heavy, and my eyelids had a mutual attraction for each other. But I thought of my canteen which I had been provident enough to fill with whiskey, and taking a good swig, I felt the generous fluid to course through every vein and fill me with fresh strength and spirit. [12]

The Graves Letters throw light on Confederate Marine uniforms too, a subject on which almost nothing else survives. Henry Graves became a lieutenant in the Confederate Marine Corps in the fall of 1862. His letters from then to the end of the war constitute a unique account of life in that branch of the service. In addition to his letters there survives a photograph of him taken in his Marine uniform at Petersburg, Virginia, late in 1863, and the uniform itself is now in the collection of Civil War relics sponsored by the Atlanta Civil War Round Table at McElreath Hall of the Atlanta Historical Society.

The Marine uniform is essentially the same as the dress uniform of the Confederate Army — sky-blue trousers, a double-breasted tunic of cadet gray with high collar and a double row of brass buttons (seven on each side). It is accented by elaborately woven epaulettes of gold braid, and the collar is marked with bars in gold braid to indicate rank. The faded sash was once crimson. The buttons are not army buttons but those manufactured by A. N. Horstmann & Allien for the "old corps," the United States Marines. They bear a design showing an eagle and a fouled anchor surmounted by a semi-circle of thirteen stars.

Henry Graves' letters indicate that the same latitude in matters of dress that marked the Confederate Army and Navy pervaded the Marine Corps also. On April 26, 1863 he wrote his mother: "The coat you sent me the sample of I shall like very much;

11. I. D. Graves to Mrs. S. D. Graves, *CSS Savannah,* June 13, 1864.
12. I. D. Graves to Mrs. S. D. Graves, James Island, S. C., January 20, 1865.

but am yet in doubt whether I want it made sack or like my dress[,] military. Just wait and I will write you when I am in need of it, and then say how to make it. . . . I got me a coat and a pair of pants the other day, made out of a sort of blue flannel, which is light and will do for the weather for a while yet. The white vests made military — I should like very much."[13]

He devoted much of his letter of November 3, 1863 to matters of dress:

> I enclose by express today to Social Circle the butter bucket with the patterns for duty coat and pants and some buttons for my overcoat and I send 18 — you can use them as you think best. [A proper overcoat would have fourteen large buttons in front and four on the tails, plus a single small button on each cuff.] If you have not already cut the coat, please cut them a little longer than Pa's coat (that black sack-looking overcoat of the raglan style is the one I mean) but which I wish them cut exactly [like] in every respect. I believe I told you about the cape; make it to meet in front, under the throat to be held up by buttons under the collar of the coat. Please make button and eyelet holes to the number of six at regular intervals down the front of the cape so that it can be buttoned up and worn at times by itself; I have buttons for the cape. If you can get it, I would like very much to have enough of the cloth for a sack coat and a pair of pants. If you have the cloth to spare now and will send it in the same bundle I will get it cut and made here. If you haven't it on hand, we will wait till I get home if I succeed in that. There is something I do want very much now, and that is some sort of cloth to make me a vest. Have you any remnants of black cloth of casimer or indeed anything that will make a vest? Or have I any winter vests at home? If not, please send me enough jeans, if you have it, for a vest.[14]

His letter of December 26 to his sister graphically illustrates the plight of any Confederate officer trying to keep himself in proper uniform on pay in grossly inflated currency. "Please say to my Father," he wrote, "that I will have to get a pair of shoes made here at once, and have no money to pay for them. They will cost me 60 dollars. If he has 50 he can spare now and will send me I can make out to pay the other ten and will be much obliged to him. My pay of $80 per month barely pays my mess bill and contributes almost nothing towards my clothing. Shoes, and inferior ones at that, are selling in town for 125 dollars; boots from 175 to 200. If the government doesn't raise my pay soon I can't imagine how I am to get along. I am almost persuaded to get married here and to go and live with the girl's father."[15]

The difficulties that beset the Graves boys are typical of the experiences of the young officers of the Confederate Army, Navy, and Marine Corps. The Confederate uniforms in museums are relics of a military service that was short-lived and that must be counted a failure in the pages of history. But these mementoes of a time past breathe the personalities and hopes, the trials and disappointments of the men who wore them.

＊　＊　＊　＊　＊

Confederate uniforms as they survive in museums and as they are recorded in photographs of individuals are our best records of the uniforms as they actually existed in

13. H. L. Graves to Mrs. S. D. Graves, Savannah, Ga., April 22, 1863 (addition dated April 26).
14. H. L. Graves to Mrs. S. D. Graves, *CSS Savannah*, November 3, 1863.
15. H. L. Graves to Cora Graves, *CSS Savannah*, December 26, 1863.

everyday Confederate life. An admirable record of those uniforms as they were intended to be, however, exists in drawings of them published by the Confederates themselves.

This volume collects three rare Confederate publications into one book: *The Uniform and Dress of the Army of the Confederate States* (Richmond: Chas. H. Wynne, 1861), *Uniform and Dress of the Navy of the Confederate States* ([Richmond: 1862?]) and its accompanying, but separately issued, set of plates. The Army volume and the set of Navy plates are published here from copies at the Library of the Boston Athenaeum through the cooperation and permission of the Athenaeum and Walter Muir Whitehill. The text to accompany the Navy plates exists in its original form only in a unique copy in the Alderman Library of the University of Virginia. It is printed here through the cooperation and permission of the University and John Cook Wyllie.

The original edition of the army volume was the idea of Colonel Blanton Duncan, an impetuous Southern sympathizer in Kentucky who early in the war joined the Confederates and removed his family from Louisville to Richmond. Duncan apparently had had prewar experience as an engraver and he spent most of his Confederate career in Columbia, South Carolina, manufacturing Confederate banknotes and bonds for the Confederate Treasury Department and publishing sheet music (as well as doing engraving for other publishers) as a private sideline.

Colonel Duncan announced the approaching publication of *The Uniform and Dress of the Army of the Confederate States* in advertisements in Southern newspapers beginning September 1, 1861:

> A limited edition. Only 1,000 copies of this work, the authorized standard, will shortly be issued.
>
> The distinction between the various grades are shown by the plates, of which there will be fifteen, and consisting of all the different departments of the service, and comprising about fifty figures. This edition will be plain black, and will be followed by another edition in full colors, a magnificent work. It contains plates, and also full directions for the guidance of tailors.[16]

The first edition came from the press sometime in the fall of 1861. It contains nine plates of full-length figures illustrating various Confederate uniforms. Additional plates illustrate badges, chevrons, and buttons. A final plate is described as the "tailor's plate." The drawings are by Ernest Crehen, a lithographer trained through his designing of labels for the products of Richmond's tobacco factories. The lithographic printing is by P. L. Valory of Petersburg. The volume was published for Colonel Blanton by Charles H. Wynne of Richmond. The original edition measures 35½ x 28 centimeters. It is bound in boards covered with marbled paper and bearing a label repeating the title enclosed in decorative borders.

Copies of the first edition are major rarities among Confederate collections. Copies of the second edition are even rarer. Though announced for publication in 1861 and though it bears that date in its imprint, the second edition could not have been issued earlier than late January of 1862. Tipped in before its first plate is a copy of the

16. Advertisement by Col. Blanton Duncan, Atlanta *Southern Confederacy,* September 1, 1861.

Confederate War Department's General Order No. 4 of January 24, 1862, announcing changes in the regulations concerning caps. Also tipped in is a strip illustrating in color the new caps. It is doubtful that more than a very few copies of the edition with colored plates were ever issued. Nashville was evacuated after the fall of Fort Donelson in mid-February 1862 and was soon occupied by Federal troops. The plates in the hands of J. T. Wagner of Nashville, the only printer in the Confederacy equipped to work in color, fell to the enemy. In this edition, plates 1, 2, 5, and 6 bear the note: "Color printing by J. T. Wagner, Nashville." Plates 3, 4, 7, and 8 are without note of the printer. Plates 7 and 8 carry the note "Lith of B. Duncan, Columbia, S. C." The other plates (9 through 15) are the same as in the first edition.

Copies of the edition with colored plates are excessively rare. Only one copy (an imperfect one) has appeared in American book auction records.[17] It sold in 1952 for $1,000 and is now part of the J. K. Lilly Library at the University of Indiana. The Confederate Museum in Richmond has a complete copy and a second set of the plates. Other complete copies are at Duke University, Emory University, and in the Paul Mellon and Raymond L. J. Riling Libraries. The Boston Athenaeum has a loose set of plates in color.

The rarity of the second edition of *The Uniform and Dress of the Army of the Confederate States* is attested in a letter from the widow of a Richmond minister written from Richmond in 1896: "My mother, who was in Richmond at the time of the evacuation, was in the War Dept. building when it was on fire, and in going out picked up this book. In a short time the building, with its contents, was consumed. I think it exceedingly improbable that another copy of this book can be obtained."[18]

In addition to the two editions with plates, Wynne published an eleven-page pamphlet reproducing the text of General Order No. 9 of June 6, 1861 without illustration. Copies of this pamphlet are in the collections of the Louisiana State University, the North Carolina Historical Commission, and the Virginia Historical Society. The text of the General Order appears also in numerous editions of the Confederate Army regulations.

As the war progressed and military niceties became less and less important, the battle dress of both sides became more and more nondescript. Confederate uniforms, especially, became, as often as not, no uniforms at all — simply what could be scrounged or captured. Supply trains of Federal armies and the bodies of dead Yankees furnished a good portion of Confederate soldier clothing. And the butternut color of Confederate homespun, produced by a dye made of copperas and walnut hulls, gradually replaced the gray of manufactured goods.

As previously mentioned, both the separate publication of the Navy uniform regulations and the plates exist only in single copies, the pamphlet at the University of

17. *American Book-Prices Current, 1951-52* (New York, 1952), p. 616.
18. Mrs. G. H. Shields to Philip Rhinelander, Richmond, Va., February 4, 1896. Letter in the Raymond L. J. Riling Library.

Virginia and the set of plates at the Boston Athenaeum. Whether or not the set of plates is complete is impossible to determine. Perhaps it should include a "tailor's plate." The Navy plates were drawn by Crehen. There is no note of their printer or publisher. They measure 37 x 28 centimeters. The pamphlet *Uniform and Dress of the Navy of the Confederate States* also bears no note of printer or publisher. It is complete in eight pages and measures 23 centimeters in height. For this new edition the Navy uniform regulations are reset in type on two pages. The Army uniform regulations and all the plates are reproduced by offset lithography.

An earlier edition of this collection of material on the Army and Navy uniforms of the Confederacy was published in an edition of four hundred numbered copies by Ray Riling and Robert Halter in 1952. Though hardly a rarity to compare to the Confederate editions, the 1952 issue of *Uniform and Dress, Army and Navy of the Confederate States* is now out of print and already a collector's item. This edition of 1960 makes available for a new group of military historians and collectors important and rare material relating to our American Civil War, that most climactic period of American military history.

*April 23, 1960*                                        RICHARD HARWELL

# UNIFORM AND DRESS

## OF THE

## OF THE

# CONFEDERATE STATES

---

ADJUTANT AND INSPECTOR GENERAL'S OFFICE,
RICHMOND, SEPTEMBER 12, 1861.

The work styled the "Uniform and Dress of the Army of the Confederate States," for which a copyright has been secured by Blanton Duncan, is published by authority.

S. COOPER,
*Adjutant and Inspector General.*

---

RICHMOND:

CHAS. H. WYNNE, PRINTER, 94 MAIN STREET.

LITHOGRAPHS BY E. CREHEN.

1861.

ADJUTANT AND INSPECTOR GENERAL'S OFFICE,
Richmond, Va., June 6, 1861.

GENERAL ORDERS,
No. 9.

# Uniform and Dress of the Army.

### TUNIC.

#### For Commissioned Officers.

1.......All Officers shall wear a tunic of gray cloth, known as cadet gray; the skirt to extend halfway between the hip and the knee; double breasted for all grades.

2.......For a *Brigadier General*—Two rows of buttons on the breast, eight in each row, placed in pairs; the distance between the rows four inches at top and three inches at bottom; stand-up collar, to rise no higher than to permit the chin to turn freely over it; to hook in front at the bottom, and slope thence up and backward, at an angle of thirty degrees, on each side; cuffs two and a half inches deep on the under side, there to be buttoned with three small buttons, and sloped upwards to a point at a distance of four inches from the end of the sleeve; pockets in the folds of the skirt, with one button at the hip and one at the end of each pocket, making four buttons on the back and skirt of the tunic, the hip buttons to range with the lowest breast buttons.

3........For a *Colonel*—the same as for a Brigadier General, except that there will be only seven buttons in each row on the breast, placed at equal distances.

4.......For a *Lieutenant Colonel, Major, Captain* and *Lieutenant*—the same as for a Colonel.

#### For Enlisted Men.

5.......The uniform coat for all enlisted men shall be a double breasted tunic of gray cloth, known as cadet gray, with the skirt extending halfway between the hip and the knee; two rows of buttons on the breast, seven in each row; the distance between the rows four inches at top and three inches at bottom; stand-up collar, to rise no higher than to permit the chin to turn freely over it; to hook in front at the bottom, and slope thence backwards at an angle of thirty degrees on each side; cuffs two and a half inches deep at the under seam, to button with two small buttons, and to be slightly pointed on the upper part of the arm; pockets in the folds of the skirts. The collars and cuffs to be of the color prescribed for facings for the respective arms of service, and the edges of the tunic to be trimmed throughout with the same colored cloth. Narrow lining in the skirts of the tunic of gray material.

### FACINGS.

6.......The facings for General Officers, and for Officers of the Adjutant General's Department, the Quartermaster General's Department, the Commissary General's Department, and the Engineers—buff. The tunic for all officers to be edged throughout with the facings designated.

7.......For the Medical Department—black.

8.......For the Artillery—red.

9.......For the Cavalry—yellow.

10.......For the Infantry—light blue.

11.......For fatigue purposes, a light gray blouse, double breasted, with two rows of small buttons, seven in each row; small, turn-over collar, may be issued to the troops.

12.......On all occasions of duty, except fatigue, and when out of quarters, the coat will be buttoned and hooked at the collar. Officers on bureau duty may wear the tunic open.

### BUTTONS.

13.......For General Officers and Officers of the General Staff—bright gilt, rounded at the edge, convex, raised eagle in the centre, with stars surrounding it; large size, one inch in exterior diameter; small size, half an inch.

14.......For Officers of the Corps of Engineers, the same as for the General Staff, except that, in place of the eagle and stars, there will be a raised E in German text.

15.......For Officers of Artillery, Infantry, Riflemen and Cavalry—gilt, convex, plain, with large raised letter in the centre: A, for the Artillery; I, for the Infantry; R, for the Riflemen; C, for the Cavalry; large size, seven-eighths of an inch in exterior diameter; small size, half an inch.

16.......Aides-de-Camp may wear the button of the General Staff, or of their regiments or corps, at their option.

17.......For enlisted men of Artillery—yellow, convex, large raised letter A in the centre; three-quarters of an inch in exterior diameter.

18.......For all other enlisted men, the same as for the Artillery, except that the number of the regiment, in large figures, will be substituted for the letter A.

### TROWSERS.

19.......The uniform trowsers for both officers and enlisted men will be of cloth throughout the year; made loose, and to spread well over the foot; of light (or sky) blue color for regimental officers and enlisted men; and of dark blue cloth for all other officers; reinforced for the Cavalry.

20.......For General Officers—two stripes of gold lace on the outer seam, one-eighth of an inch apart, and each five-eighths of an inch in width.

21.......For Officers of the Adjutant General's Department, the Quartermaster General's Department, the Commissary General's Department, and the Corps of Engineers—one stripe of gold lace on the outer seam, one inch and a quarter in width.

22.......For the Medical Department—a black velvet stripe, one inch and a quarter in width, with a gold cord on each edge of the stripe.

23.......For Regimental Officers—a stripe of cloth on the outer seam, one inch and a quarter in width; color according to corps: for Artillery, red; Cavalry, yellow; Infantry, dark blue.

24.......For the non-commissioned staff of regiments and for all sergeants, a stripe of cotton webbing or braid on the outer seam, one and a quarter inch in width; color according to arm of service.

25.......For all other enlisted men—plain.

### CHAPEAU, OR COCKED HAT.

26.......A chapeau, or cocked hat, will be worn by General Officers and Officers of the General Staff and Corps of Engineers, of what is called the French pattern; the model to be deposited in the office of the Quartermaster General.

27.......Forage cap for officers—a cap similar in form to that known as the French kepi, according to pattern to be deposited in the office of the Quartermaster General.

28.......Uniform cap—according to pattern to be deposited in the office of the Quartermaster General.

### POMPON.

29.......For the Artillery—red.

30.......For the Infantry—light blue.

31.......For the Cavalry—yellow.

### CRAVAT, OR STOCK.

32.......For all officers—black. When a cravat is worn, the tie not to be visible at the opening of the collar.

33.......For enlisted men—black leather, according to pattern.

### BOOTS.

34........For all officers—ankle or Jefferson.

35........For enlisted men of Cavalry—ankle and Jefferson, according to pattern.

36........For other enlisted men—Jefferson, according to pattern.

### SPURS.

37........For all mounted officers—yellow metal or gilt.

38.......For enlisted mounted men—yellow metal, according to pattern.

### GLOVES.

39.......For General Officers, and Officers of the General Staff and Staff Corps—buff or white.

40.......For officers of Artillery, Infantry and Cavalry—white.

### SASH.

41.......For General Officers—buff silk net, with silk bullion fringe ends; sash to go twice around the waist, and to tie behind the left hip; pendent part not to extend more than eighteen inches below the tie.

42.......For officers of the General Staff and Engineers, and of the Artillery and Infantry—red silk net. For officers of the Cavalry—yellow silk net. For medical officers—green silk net. All with silk bullion fringe ends; to go around the waist, and to tie as for General Officers.

43.......For Sergeants—of worsted, with worsted bullion fringe ends: red for Artillery and Infantry, and yellow for Cavalry. To go twice around the waist, and to tie as above specified.

### SWORD BELT.

44.......For all officers—a waist belt, not less than one and one-half inches, nor more than two inches wide; to be worn over the sash; the sword to be suspended from it by slings of the same material as the belt, with a hook attached to the belt upon which the sword may be hung.

45.......For General Officers—Russian leather, with three stripes of gold embroidery; the slings embroidered on both sides.

46.......For all other officers—black leather, plain.

47.......For all non-commissioned officers—black leather, plain.

### SWORD BELT PLATE.

48.......For all officers and enlisted men—gilt, rectangular; two inches wide, with a raised bright rim; a silver wreath of laurel encircling the "arms of the Confederate States."

### SWORD AND SCABBARD.

49.......For all officers—according to patterns to be deposited in the Ordnance Bureau.

### SWORD KNOT.

50.......For all officers—of plaited leather, with tassels.

### BADGES TO DISTINGUISH RANK.

51.......On the sleeve of the tunic, rank will be distinguished by an ornament of gold braid, (in form as represented in the drawing,) extending around the seam of the cuff, and up the outside of the arm to the bend of the elbow. To be of one braid for lieutenants; two, for captains; three, for field officers; and four, for general officers. The braid to be one-eighth of an inch in width.

52.......On the front part of the collar of the tunic, the rank of officers will be distinguished as follows:

53.......*General Officers*—A wreath, with three stars enclosed, embroidered in gold. The edge of the wreath to be three-fourths of an inch from the front edge of the collar; the stars to be arranged horizontally; the centre one to be one and one-fourth inches in exterior diameter, and the others three-fourths of an inch.

54........*Colonel*—Three stars, embroidered in gold, arranged horizontally, and dividing equally the vertical space of the collar. Each star to be one and one-fourth inches in exterior diameter;

the front star to be three-fourths of an inch from the edge of the collar.

55.......*Lieutenant Colonel*—Two stars of same material, size and arrangement as for a colonel.

56.......*Major*—One star of same material and size as for a colonel; to be placed three-fourths of an inch from edge of collar, and dividing equally the vertical space.

57.......*Captain*—Three horizontal bars, embroidered in gold; each one-half inch in width; the upper bar to be three inches in length; the front edge of the bars to incline to correspond with the angle of the collar, and to be three-fourths of an inch from the edge; the line of the back edges to be vertical.

58.......*First Lieutenant*—Two horizontal bars of same material and size as for captains, and dividing equally the vertical space of collar.

59.......*Second Lieutenant*—One horizontal bar of same material and size as for the centre bar of captain, and dividing equally the vertical space of collar.

### OVERCOATS FOR ENLISTED MEN.

60.......For mounted men—of cadet gray cloth; stand-up collar; double breasted; cape to reach to the cuff of the coat, when the arm is extended, and to button all the way up, (buttons, eighteen.)

61.......For footmen—of cadet gray cloth; stand-up collar; double breasted; cape to reach to the elbows, when the arm is extended, and to button all the way up, (buttons, eighteen.) For the present, to be a talma, with sleeves, of water-proof material; black.

### CHEVRONS.

62.......The rank of non-commissioned officers will be marked by chevrons on both sleeves of the uniform tunic and the overcoat, above the elbow, of silk or worsted binding, half an inch wide; color the same as the edging of the tunic; points down, as follows:

63.......For a *Sergeant Major*—three bars and an arc in silk.

64.......For a *Quartermaster Sergeant*—three bars and a tie in silk.

65.......For an *Ordnance Sergeant*—three bars and a star in silk.

66.......For a *First* (or *Orderly*) *Sergeant*—three bars and a lozenge in worsted.

67.......For a *Sergeant*—three bars in worsted.

68.......For a *Corporal*—two bars in worsted.

### HAIR AND BEARD.

69.......The hair to be short; the beard to be worn at the pleasure of the individual; but, when worn, to be kept short and neatly trimmed.

BY COMMAND OF THE SECRETARY OF WAR:

S. COOPER,
*Adjutant and Inspector General.*

## MEMORANDUM AS EXPLANATION OF THE PLATES, REGARDING COLORS, BADGES OF RANK, &c.

GENERAL—Buff collar, cuff and edging to tunic. Four rows of braid on sleeve; eight pairs of buttons; wreath around stars. Dark blue trowsers, with two stripes of gold lace, each five-eighths of an inch wide, and one-eighth apart, on the outer seam. Sash, buff silk net.

COLONELS OF THE STAFF—Seven buttons; three rows of braid; three stars on each side of collar. One stripe of gold lace, one and a quarter inches wide, on trowsers. Sash, red silk net. Facings, buff.

LIEUTENANT COLONEL AND MAJOR OF THE STAFF—Same as Colonel, except two stars for Lieutenant Colonel and one star for Major.

SURGEON—Facings, black. One star on collar. On trowsers, black velvet stripe, one and a quarter inches wide, with gold cord on each edge. Sash, green silk net.

ARTILLERY—Red collar, cuffs and edging to tunic. Red stripe of cloth on outer seam of trowsers, one and a quarter inches wide. Red band around cap. Stars or bars and braid, according to rank. Sash, red silk net.

CAVALRY—Yellow collar, cuffs and edging to tunic. Yellow stripe of cloth on trowsers. Yellow band on cap. Sash, yellow silk net.

INFANTRY—Light blue collar, cuffs and edging to tunic. Dark blue stripe of cloth on trowsers. Light blue band on cap. Sash, red silk net.

2

GENERAL

ADJUTANT GENERAL
COLONEL

STAFF

COLONEL
OF ENGINEERS

LITH. DRAWING BY E. CREHEN, RICHMOND

APPROVED BY WAR DEPARTMENT

LITH. PRINTING BY VALDRY PETERSBURG VA

QUARTERMASTER G.nl

COLONÈL

STAFF

SURGEON

MAJOR

LITH. DRAWING BY E. CREHEN · RICHMOND

APPROVED BY WAR DEPARTMENT

LITH PRINTING BY VALDRY PETERSBURG VA

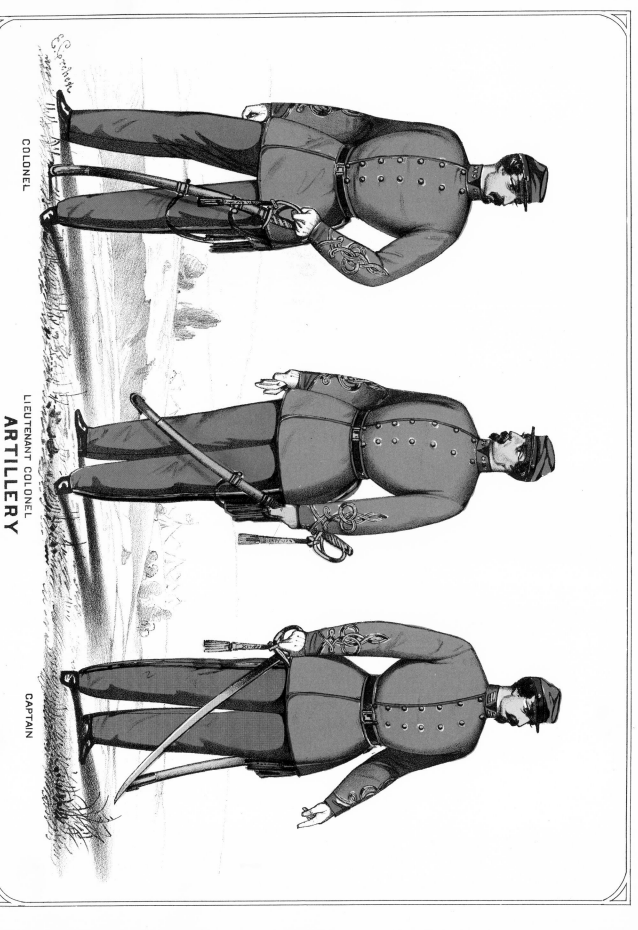

LITH. DRAWING BY E. CREHEN . RICHMOND

APPROVED BY WAR DEPARTMENT

LITH PRINTING BY VALORY PETERSBURG VA

COLONEL

LIEUTENANT COLONEL
**ARTILLERY**

CAPTAIN

LITH. DRAWING BY E. CREHEN. RICHMOND

SERGEANT

PRIVATE

**ARTILLERY**

MUSICIAN

APPROVED BY WAR DEPARTMENT

LITH. PRINTING BY VALORY PETERSBURG VA.

LITH.DRAWING BY E.CREHEN. RICHMOND

COLONEL

MAJOR

CAPTAIN

# CAVALRY

APPROVED BY WAR DEPARTMENT

LITH PRINTING BY VALORY PETERSBURG VA

SERGEANT

PRIVATE

**CAVALRY**

MUSICIAN

LITH. DRAWING BY E.CREHEN. RICHMOND

APPROVED BY WAR DEPARTMENT

LITH PRINTING BY VALORY PETERSBURG VA.

COLONEL

CAPTAIN

FIRST LIEUTENANT

# INFANTRY

APPROVED BY WAR DEPARTMENT

SERGEANT

PRIVATE

MUSICIAN

# INFANTRY

APPROVED BY WAR DEPARTMENT

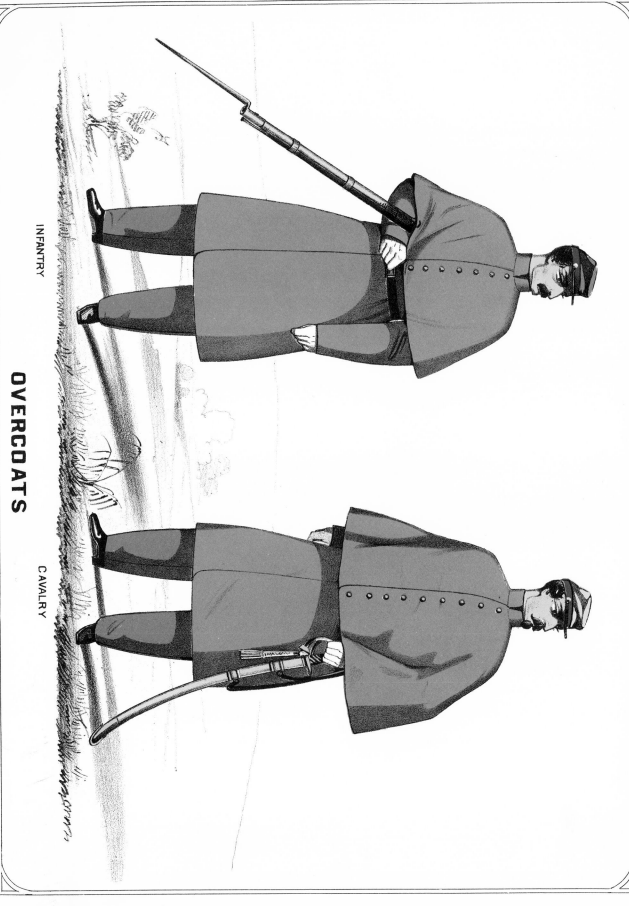

LITH. DRAWING BY E. CREHEN . RICHMOND

INFANTRY

**OVERCOATS**

APPROVED BY WAR DEPARTMENT

CAVALRY

LITH PRINTING BY VALORY PETERSBURG VA

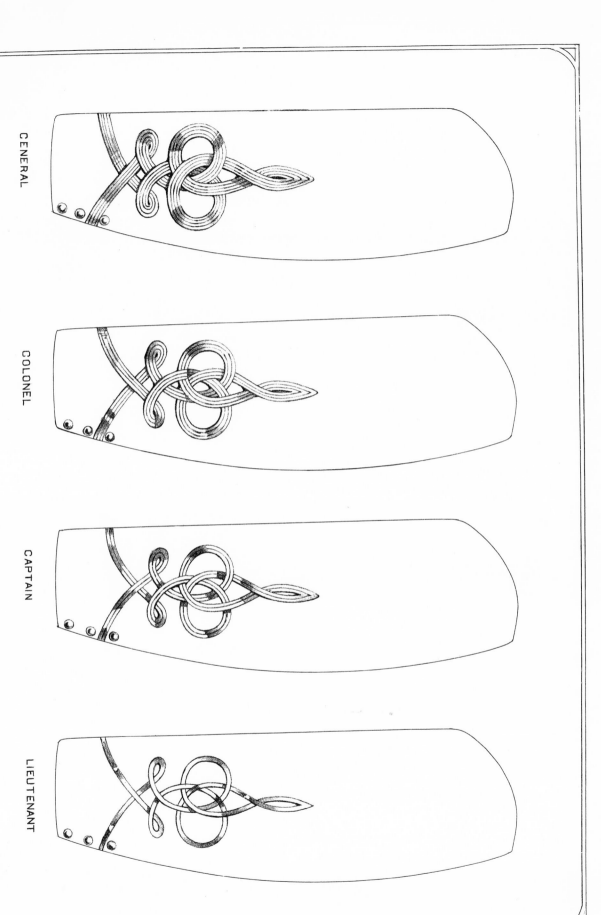

**BADGES**

CENERAL

COLONEL

CAPTAIN

LIEUTENANT

LITH. DRAWING BY E. CREHEN. RICHMOND

APPROVED BY WAR DEPARTMENT

LITH. PRINTING BY VALORY. PETERSBURG VA.

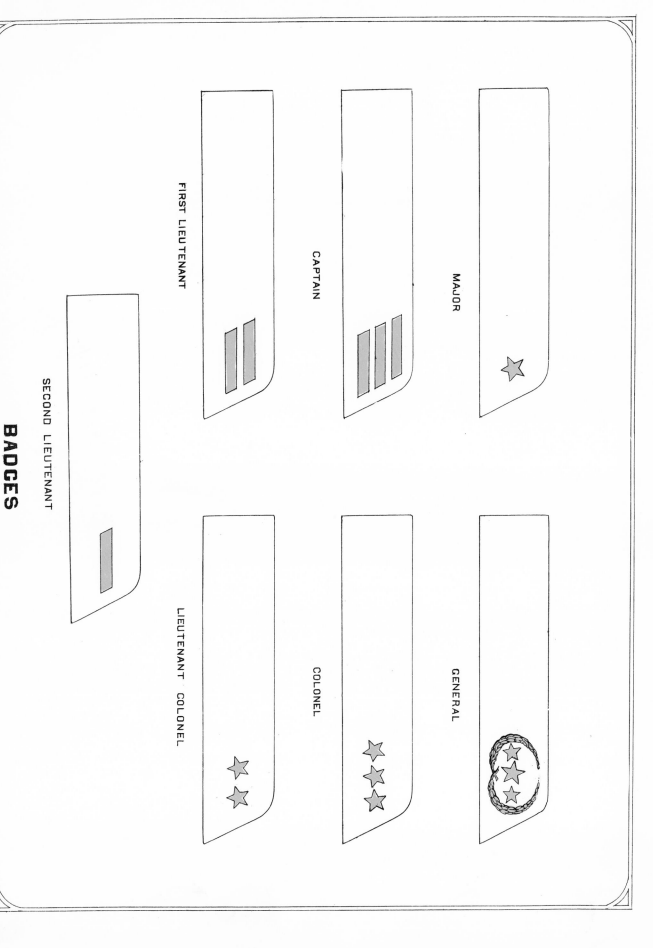

BADGES

FIRST LIEUTENANT

CAPTAIN

MAJOR

SECOND LIEUTENANT

LIEUTENANT COLONEL

COLONEL

GENERAL

LITH. DRAWING BY E. CREHEN . RICHMOND

ORDNANCE SERGEANT

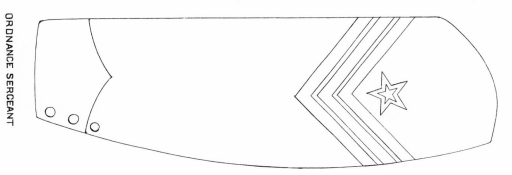

QUARTERMASTER SERGEANT

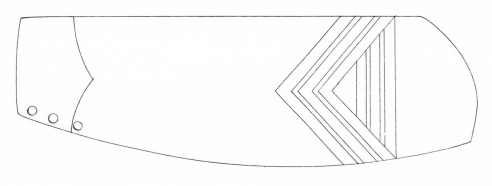

# CHEVRONS

APPROVED BY WAR DEPARTMENT

SERGEANT MAJOR

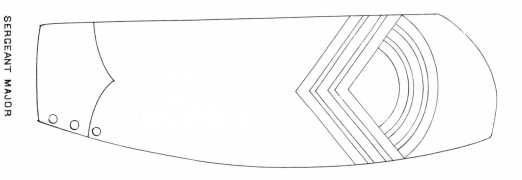

LITH PRINTING BY VALORY PETERSBURG VA

LITH. DRAWING BY E.CREHEN . RICHMOND

CORPORAL
ARTILLERY

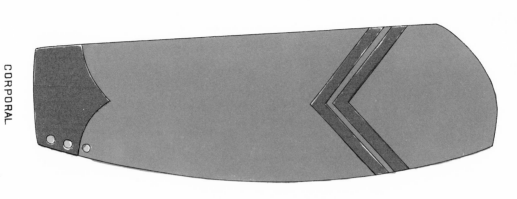

**CHEVRONS**

APPROVED BY WAR DEPARTMENT

SERGEANT
CAVALRY

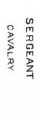

FIRST SERGEANT
INFANTRY

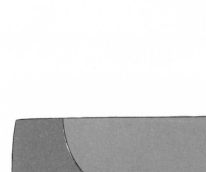

LITH PRINTING BY VALORY PETERSBURG VA

LITH. DRAWING BY E. CREHEN. RICHMOND

APPROVED BY WAR DEPARTMENT

# BUTTONS

LITH. PRINTING BY VALORY PETERSBURG. VA

RIFLEMEN

GENERAL

FOR OFFICERS

ENGENEER

CAVALRY

FOR PRIVATE

ARTILLERY

ARTILLERY

INFANTRY

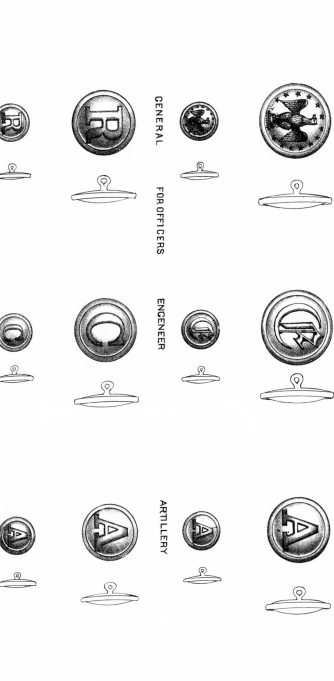

# TAILOR'S PLATE

LITH. DRAWING BY E. CREHEN. RICHMOND

APPROVED BY WAR DEPARTMENT

LITH. PRINTING BY VALDRY PETERSBURG VA

# WAR DEPARTMENT,
### Adjutant and Inspector General's Office,
*Richmond, January 24, 1862.*

GENERAL ORDERS, }
     No. 4 }

The following Regulation is published for the information of all concerned:

*Forage Cap for the Army of the Confederate States.*

Pattern—Of the form known as the French *kepi;* to be made of cloth.

For General Officers, and Officers of the General Staff and Engineers—Dark blue band, sides and crown.

For the Artillery—Dark blue band; sides and crown red.

For the Infantry—Dark blue band; sides and crown light blue.

For the Cavalry—Dark blue band; sides and crown yellow.

*Marks to distinguish Rank.*

Four gold braids for General Officers; three for Field Officers; two for Captains, and one for Lieutenants, to extend from the band on the front, back and both sides to the top of the cap—and the centre of the crown to be embroidered with the same number of braids.

For enlisted men—The cap will be of the same pattern; the band to be dark blue, and, as in the case of officers, the several arms of service will be designated by the color of the sides and crown—Red for Artillery; light blue for Infantry, and yellow for Cavalry. The number of the Regiment will be worn in front, in yellow metal.

In hot weather, a white duck, or linen cover, known as a havelock, will be worn—the apron to fall behind, so as to protect the ears and neck from the rays of the sun. In winter, in bad weather, an oil skin cover will be worn, with an apron to fall over the coat collar.

By command of the Secretary of War.

## S. COOPER,
*Adjutant and Inspector General.*

GENERAL       COL       CAP<sup>T</sup>       LIEU<sup>T</sup>

            CAVALRY      INFANTRY      ARTILLERY

PUBLISHER'S NOTE:

    *The original work of "Uniforms and Dress of the Army of the Confederate States" of 1861, was nearly completed by the printers when an official order was issued specifying changes in the braiding or markings of the caps. This fact was proclaimed in an official errata sheet which was inserted in the original release. The above four small illustrations accompanied the brief errata to guide the reader.*

    *To enable present day collectors and students to more accurately note these cap changes we have included the above General Orders No. 4, of January 24, 1862.*

# NAVY

# UNIFORM AND DRESS

## OF THE

## *NAVY OF THE CONFEDERATE STATES*

### Undress [Sea Officers] Coat.

*For a Flag Officer,* shall be a frock coat of steel grey cloth, faced with the same and lined with black silk serge, double breasted, with two rows of large navy buttons on the breast, nine in each row, placed four inches and a half apart from eye to eye at top, and two inches and a half at bottom. Rolling collar, skirts to be full, commencing at the top of the hip bone and descending four-fifths thence towards the knee, with one button behind on each hip and one near the bottom of each fold. The cuffs to be two inches and a half deep, with one strip of gold lace one-half an inch wide below the seam, but joining it; three strips of lace of the same width on the sleeves above the cuffs, separated by a space of three-eighths of an inch from each other, the upper one with a loop three inches long, and a strip of lace half an inch wide, from the lower button to the end of the cuffs on the upper side of the opening, and four small sized buttons (navy buttons) in the opening.

*For a Captain,* the same as for a Flag Officer, except that there shall be but three strips of lace around the sleeve and cuff, including the looped strip.

*For a Commander,* the same in all respects as for a Captain, except that there shall be but two strips of lace around the sleeve and cuff, including the looped strip, and three small buttons in the opening.

*For a Lieutenant,* the same in all respects as for a Commander, except that the cuffs shall have but one strip of gold lace, looped, around the upper edge.

*For a Master,* the same as for a Lieutenant, except that the cuffs shall have but one strip of lace one-fourth of an inch wide, without a loop, around the upper edge.

*For a Passed Midshipman,* the same as for a Master, excepting that the cuffs shall have, instead of lace, three medium sized navy buttons around the upper edge.

*For a Midshipman,* the same as for a Passed Midshipman, except that medium sized buttons shall be substituted for the large buttons.

### Undress [Civil Officers] Coat.

*For a Surgeon* of over twelve years' standing, shall be a frock coat of steel grey cloth, faced with the same, double breasted, rolling collar, with two rows of large navy buttons on the breast, nine in each row, proportioned for body and skirts the same as for a captain, skirts lined with black silk serge, one button behind on each hip, and one near the bottom of each fold of the skirts. Cuffs the same as for a commander, except that a plain strip of lace shall be substituted for the loop.

*For a Surgeon* of less than twelve years' standing, the same, except that there shall be one strip of lace around the cuff and sleeve.

*For a Passed Assistant Surgeon,* the same as for a Surgeon of less than twelve years' standing, except that the lace on the cuff shall be one-quarter of an inch wide.

*For an Assistant Surgeon,* the same as for a Surgeon, except that instead of lace there shall be three medium sized buttons on the cuff.

*For a Paymaster* of over twelve years' standing, the same as

prescribed for a Surgeon over twelve years.

*For a Paymaster* of less than twelve years' standing, the same as for a Surgeon of less than twelve years.

*For a Chief Engineer* of more than twelve years' standing, the same as for a Surgeon of more than twelve years.

*For a First Assistant Engineer,* the same as for a Chief Engineer, except that there shall be but one strip of lace on the cuff one-quarter of an inch wide.

*For a Second and Third Assistant,* the same as for a First Assistant Engineer, except that instead of lace the cuffs shall have three medium sized buttons around the upper edge.

*For a Chaplain,* the same as for a Surgeon, except that it shall be single breasted, with one row of nine large navy buttons on the breast. The cuffs plain with three small buttons in the opening.

*For a Professor and Commodore's Secretary,* the same as for a Chaplain, except that there shall be but eight buttons on the breast.

*For a Clerk,* the same as for a Secretary, except that there shall be but six buttons on the breast.

### Vest.

*For all officers,* steel grey or white, single breasted, standing collar, with nine small buttons in front, and not to show below the coat.

### Pantaloons.

*For all officers,* shall be of steel grey cloth or white drill, made loose to spread well over the foot and to be worn over boots or shoes.

### Shoulder Straps.

*For a Flag Officer,* of sky-blue cloth, edged with black, four inches long and one inch and three-eighths wide, bordered with an embroidery of gold one-quarter of an inch in width, with four stars in line at equal distances, the two on the ends six-tenths of an inch in diameter, and the two intermediate six-eighths of an inch in diameter.

*For a Captain,* the same as for a Flag Officer, except that there shall be three stars at equal distances, each six-tenths of an inch in diameter.

*For a Commander,* the same as for a Captain, except that there shall be but two stars.

*For a Lieutenant,* the same as for a Commander, except that there shall be but one star, in the centre.

*For a Master,* the same as for a Lieutenant, except that there shall be no star.

*For a Passed Midshipman,* a strip of gold lace four inches long and half an inch wide.

*For a Surgeon* of more than twelve years' standing, the same as for a Master, except that they shall be of black cloth, with two sprigs of olive, crossed, embroidered in gold in the centre.

*For a Surgeon* of less than twelve years' standing, the same, except that there shall be but one sprig of olive.

*For a passed Assistant Surgeon,* the same as for a Surgeon, except that instead of sprigs of olive, there shall be an olive leaf embroidered in gold on each end.

*For an Assistant Surgeon,* the same as for a Passed Assistant Surgeon, without the leaves.

*For a Paymaster,* of more than twelve years' standing, the same as for a Surgeon of more than twelve years, except that the straps shall be of dark green cloth.

*For a Paymaster,* of less than twelve years standing, the same as for a Surgeon of less than twelve years, except that the straps shall be of dark green cloth.

*For an Assistant Paymaster,* the same as for an Assistant Surgeon, except that the straps shall be of dark green cloth.

*For a Chief Engineer* of more than twelve years standing, the same as for a Master, except that there shall be two sprigs of live oak embroidered in gold in the centre, and the straps shall be of dark blue cloth.

*For a Chief Engineer* of less than twelve years' standing, the same, except that there shall be but one sprig of live oak.

### CAPS.

Cap of steel gray cloth, to be not less than three inches and a half, nor more than four inches in height, and not more than ten nor less than nine inches and a half at top, with patent leather visor, to be worn by all officers in service dress.

*For a Flag Officer,* the device shall be a foul anchor in an open wreath of live oak leaves, with four stars above the anchor, embroidered in gold as per pattern, on the front of the cap above a band of gold lace one inch and three quarters wide.

*For a Captain,* the same as for a flag officer, except that there shall be but three stars above the anchor, and the gold band shall be one and one half inches wide.

*For a Commander,* the same as for Captain, except that there shall be but two stars.

*For a Lieutenant,* the same as for a Commander, except that there shall be but one star.

*For a Master,* the same as for a Lieutenant, except that there shall be no star.

*For a Passed Midshipman,* a foul anchor without the wreath.

*For a Surgeon,* of over twelve years standing, a wreath of olive leaves with three stars, four tenths of an inch in diameter, embroidered in gold as per pattern, on the front of the cap, above a band of gold lace one inch and a quarter wide.

*For a Surgeon,* of less than twelve years standing, the same, except that there shall be two stars.

*For a Passed Assistant Surgeon,* the same as for a Surgeon, except that there shall be but one star.

*For an Assistant Surgeon,* the same as for a Surgeon, except that there shall be no star.

*For a Paymaster,* of over twelve years' standing, the same as for a Surgeon of over twelve years standing.

*For a Paymaster,* of less than twelve years, the same as for a Surgeon of less than twelve years.

*For an Assistant Paymaster,* the same as for an Assistant Surgeon.

*For a Chief Engineer,* of more than twelve years' standing, the same as for a Surgeon of more than twelve years, except that the letter E in the old English character shall be embroidered in gold below the stars.

*For a Chief Engineer,* of less than twelve years, the same, except that there shall be but two stars.

*For Second and Third Assistant Engineers,* the same as for a First Assistant Engineer, except that there shall be no stars.

### BUTTONS.

Buttons shall be of three sizes: large, medium, and small, and all of the same device, as per pattern.

### SUMMER FROCK COAT.

In summer or in tropical climates, officers may wear frock coats and pantaloons of steel grey summer cloth of the style and pattern herein prescribed, with medium size navy buttons.

### JACKETS.

May be worn as service dress by all officers when at sea, except when at general muster. To be of steel gray cloth or white drill linen with the same, double breasted, rolling collar, same number of small sized buttons on breast as for undress coat, open fly sleeve with four small buttons in the opening, with shoulder straps for appropriate grades.

### STRAW HATS.

In summer or in tropical climates, officers may also wear, except at general muster, white straw hats. The body of the hat to be six inches in height, and the rim three and a half inches in width.

### OVER COATS.

For all officers, shall be of steel gray cloth, double breasted, rolling collar, skirts to descend three inches below the knee, the same number of navy buttons, and similarly arranged as for undress coat. No buttons to be worn on the cuffs or pocket flaps. Officers entitled to shoulder straps will wear the same on their overcoats as directed for undress coats. Gray cloth cloaks may be worn in boats.

### DRESS FOR PETTY OFFICERS AND CREW.

Boatswain's Mates, Gunner's Mates, Carpenter's Mates, Sailmaker's Mates, Ship's Steward and Ship's Cook, will wear embroidered in black silk on the right sleeve of their gray jackets above the elbow in front, a foul anchor of not more than three inches length. The same device embroidered blue to be worn on the sleeves of their white frocks in summer.

All other petty officers except officers' stewards and yeomen will wear the same device on their left sleeves.

The outside clothing for petty officers, firemen and coal-heavers, seamen, ordinary seamen, landsmen and boys for muster, shall consist of gray cloth jackets and trousers, or gray woolen frocks with white duck cuffs and collars, black hats, black silk neckerchiefs and shoes, or boots in cold weather. In warm weather it shall consist of white frocks and trousers, black or white hats, as the commander may for the occasion direct, having proper regard for the comfort of the crew; black silk neckerchiefs and shoes. The collars and cuffs to be lined with blue cotton cloth, and stitched round with thread. Thick gray caps without visors may be worn by the crew at sea, except on holidays or at muster.

*For a Boatswain, Gunner, Carpenter and Sailmaker,* shall be of steel gray cloth, lined with the same; rolling collar, double breasted, two rows of large navy buttons on the breast, eight in each row; pointed pocket flaps, with three large buttons underneath each, showing one-half their diameter; three medium size buttons around each cuff, and two small ones in each opening; one button behind on each hip; one in the middle of each fold, and one in each fold near the bottom of the skirt. On each side of the collar to have one loop of three-quarters wide gold lace, to show one inch and a half wide, and four inches long, with a small size navy button in the point of each loop.

FLAG OFFICER        CAPTAIN        LIEUTENANT        SURGEON

# UNIFORMS OF THE C.S NAVY

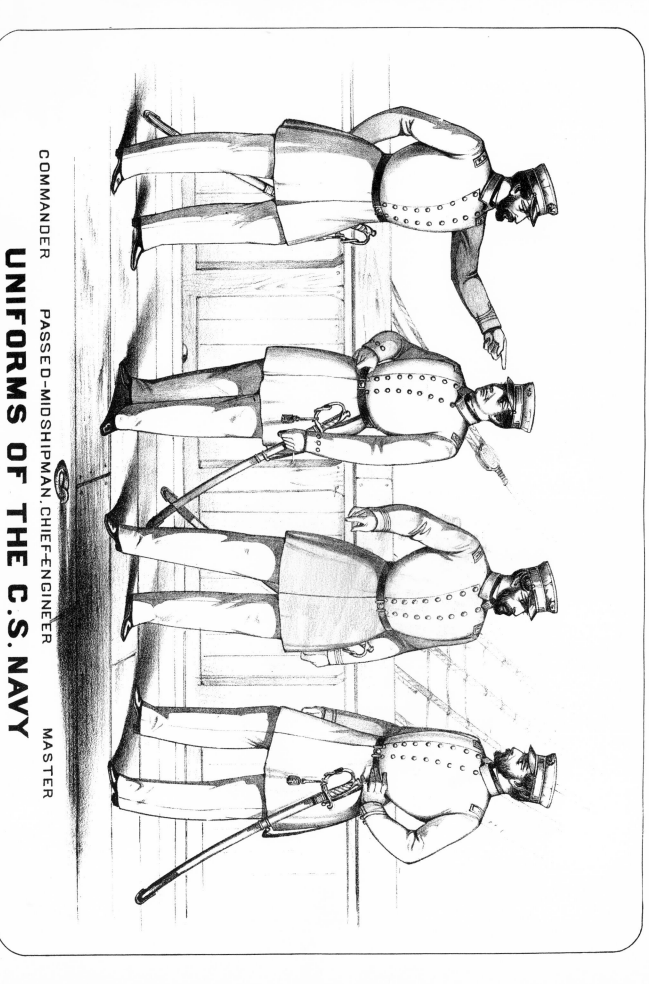

UNIFORMS OF THE C.S. NAVY

COMMANDER          PASSED-MIDSHIPMAN, CHIEF-ENGINEER          MASTER

Lith by E Crehen Richmond Va

UNIFORMS OF THE C.S NAVY

PURSER     CHAPLAIN     COMMANDERS SECRETARY     MIDSHIPMAN

Lith by E Crehen Richmond Va

# SHOULDER STRAPS

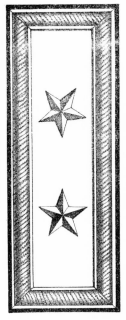

COMMANDERS

CAPTAINS

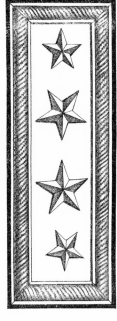

FLAG OFFICERS

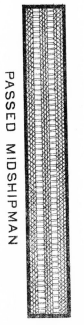

PASSED MIDSHIPMAN

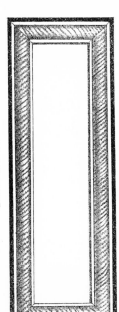

MASTER

LIEUTENANTS

# SHOULDER STRAPS

SURGEON OF OVER 12 YEARS

SURGEON OF UNDER 12 YEARS

PASSED ASSIST SURGEON

CHIEF ENGINEER OF OVER 12 YEARS

ASSISTANT SURGEON

CHIEF ENGINEER OF UNDER 12 YEARS

ASSISTANT PAYMASTER

PAYMASTER OF UNDER 12 YEARS

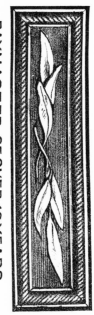

PAYMASTER OF OVER 12 YEARS

# CUFFS

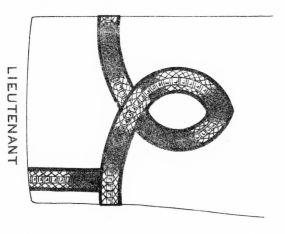

LIEUTENANT

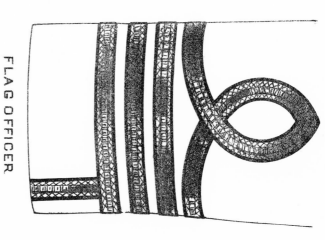

FLAG OFFICER

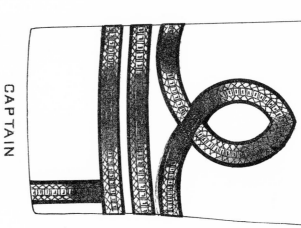

CAPTAIN

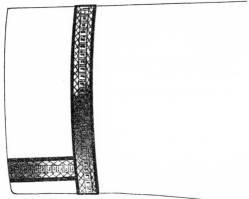

MASTER

COMMANDER

# CAP ORNAMENTS

FLAG OFFICER

CAPTAIN

COMMANDER

PASSED MIDSHIPMAN

MASTER

LIEUTENANT

# CAP ORNAMENTS & BUTTONS

SURGEON OF OVER 12 YEARS

SURGEON OF UNDER 12 YEARS

MEDIUM

LARGE

SMALL

PASS.ᴰ ASS.ᵀ SURGEON

ASS.ᵀ SURGEON

*2000 copies have been printed
by offset lithography at The Meriden Gravure
Company, Meriden, Connecticut.*

*Of these, 50 copies have been specially
bound, signed, and numbered.*